Mademoiselle Duchesne

Mademoiselle Duchesne

Mere Duchesne, RSCJ

Theresa Riley Shaw

MADEMOISELLE DUCHESNE
MERE DUCHESNE, RSCJ

iUniverse books may be ordered through booksellers or by contacting:

iUniverse
1663 Liberty Drive
Bloomington, IN 47403
www.iuniverse.com
1-800-Authors (1-800-288-4677)

ISBN: 978-1-5320-5691-8 (sc)
ISBN: 978-1-5320-5692-5 (e)

Library of Congress Control Number: 2018910783

Print information available on the last page.

iUniverse rev. date: 11/05/2018

*R*ose Philippine Duchesne was born in Grenoble, the beautiful gateway to the French Alps, in 1769. She was one of eight children born to Pierre-Francois Duchesne, a lawyer and member of the French Parliament, and Rose Euphrosine Périer, a wonderful wife and mother. Madame Duchesne taught her children to know, love, and serve God and to care for their home and small children.

Uncle Claude Périer, Madame Duchesne's brother, moved into a home next to the Duchesnes when Philippine was ten years old. Only a doorway separated the courtyards of the two households. There were babies and children everywhere. They were gently trained in obedience and self-control, along with courtesy and consideration for others.

During the terrible floods of 1778, both families were active in helping the victims. Mademoiselle Sophie and later Madame Luc tutored Philippine; her cousin Josephine Périer; the Périer boys, Augustin and Casmir; and Camille Jordan, another cousin. Their studies included Latin and Greek.

Stories of Jesuit missionaries who visited the Duchesne family thrilled Philippine. When Philippine was twelve years old, she went to the Visitation convent, Ste. Marie d'en Haut, to study for her First Holy Communion. She consecrated herself to God. That was the happiest day of her life.

Returning home again, she continued her studies with her cousins, who would remain very close to her all their lives, especially Josephine, who became Madame de Savoye-Rollin. Philippine loved to climb mountains, hike with her cousins, and read about the lives of the saints, especially the martyrs.

At eighteen years of age, Philippine went to Ste. Marie d'en Haut and asked to join the Sisters of the Visitation. Her

father, a Freemason, did not approve of her decision at first, but he eventually began to realize how happy Philippine was. He attended her reception of the black habit, white veil, and coif (a special collar) of a Visitation novice.

The French Revolution was escalating, and Catholic monasteries and convents were endangered. Philippine's father, Pierre Francois, insisted that Philippine not take her final vows but return home to Grâne, the family summer château, where she would be safer. There, also seeking safety and shelter, were her parents; her younger brother Hippolyte; and her sisters, Euphrosine, Adelaide, Mélanie, and Amélie, who also brought her two little boys.

The revolutionary government outlawed any and all religious congregations, so all convents, monasteries, and Catholic schools were closed. Many priests were imprisoned and killed. Philippine kept very busy teaching her cousins, visiting the sick, and teaching catechism to the poor children she met in the streets. During the Reign of Terror, not just the French Revolution, schools and all orphanages were closed, and hundreds of children ran the streets, many living like animals. Of the priests who were arrested, many were sent to the old monastery, Ste. Marie, which had become a prison. Philippine visited the priests there, praying with the men, nursing them, and sometimes even burying them.

At the Périer home, Philippine talked with her cousin Augustin; read to Scipion, who had weak eyes; visited with Casimir, who was just home from college; and tutored the boys with lessons, along with Camille Jordan, son of Philippine's mother's twin sister, Marie Elizabeth. She played with the little ones and attended Mass in the living room of Dr. Gagnon's house, where the Grand meets the Place Grenette. She spent many hours with Josephine (Madame de Savoye-Rollin) in works of charity.

At his summer home in Vizille, a magnificent château, Uncle Claude Périer hosted the meeting where the Tennis Court Oath opened the French Revolution. There, 463 delegates protested against existing conditions in the country and stated the need for reforms, financial and political, for which there was a crying need throughout France. This mémoire, or remonstrance to the king, was prepared by Pierre-Francois Duchesne and deliberated on by all the assembled until three o'clock in the morning on July 2, 1788. The seed for a mighty revolution had been planted. As the Reign of Terror continued, King Louis XVI was executed. Uncle Augustin Périer was made commandant of the National Guard.

Cousin Julie Tranchand, a Visitation nun from the monastery at Romans, joined the Duchesne and Périer families at Grâne. Julie and Philippine at once devised a way of life for themselves, patterned as closely as possible on that of the cloister they had left. They rose early, made morning meditation, recited their office, said the sisters' prayers, kept the fasts prescribed, and observed the rules of the Visitation nuns as far as they could. Later at Grâne, she helped Amélie with her little boys, six and three years of age. She spent time with Mélanie, her little sister, and helped with the household chores.

Many fugitive priests found their way to the Duchesne home during this period. One was the Abbé Poidebord, who acted as a manager and superintendent of construction at the textile factory for Monsieur Duchesne, Philippine's father. He resided with the Duchesnes, gave religious instructions to the younger members, and held spiritual conferences with Philippine and Julie Tranchard. He also would secretly offer Mass and give Holy Communion to those who could keep a secret. Because Pierre-Francois Duchesne was active in the French Revolution, no one suspected that kind of activity was going on in his household.

By this time in France, people had to be addressed as Citoyen or Citoyenne, not Monsieur, Madame, or Mademoiselle, as before. Much to her companion's surprise, one day Philippine brought a dying woman to their home, placed her in her own bed, and then went to get a priest for her. The woman died in the arms of Citoyenne Duchesne.

After the Concordat of 1801, things got a little better in Grenoble, and Philippine was able to persuade her family to buy the old, war-torn, and abandoned Ste. Marie d'en Haute monastery. With the help of many of the little boys she taught on the street, Philippine moved back into the monastery. She and her companion, Madame Faucherand, tried to fix up the windows, cracked walls, and leaking roof. Philippine was happiest when she was sweeping the rubble in the rooms of her beloved monastery, shoveling snow, mopping up water, or trying to repair windowpanes, the most thankless task of all, for the paste froze immediately as it was put on and would stick and try her patience.

Inspired by the great Saint Teresa of Avila, she offered every effort as a prayer. The building remained cold and drafty. Families who had remained faithful to the church sent their daughters anyway. In no time, there were thirty students, boarders, and novices (girls studying to become sisters).

A priest friend, Father Joseph Desire Varin, told Mother Madeline Sophie Barat about Philippine and her ladies of mercy, whose purpose was to bring material and spiritual help to priests hiding and those in prison, as well as instructing many children and trying to rebuild a religious foundation.

Father Varin wrote Mother Barat in 1804, "If she were alone and at the most remote corner of the world, you should go after her." He felt that Philippine wanted to do the same work as Mother Barat and that they would get along very well. They would become very special friends in Christ for the rest of their

lives. Philippine was thirty-five years old; Mother Barat was only twenty-five years old.

Philippine and several of her companions became postulants in this new society under the direction of Mother Barat. One day, each sister would take the vows of poverty, chastity, and obedience and dedicate their lives to the education of youth until death.

In Amiens in 1800, Mother Madeline Sophie Barat had begun her new society of religious, which was dedicated to teaching youth about Jesus Christ and His loving, forgiving, and saving heart. They would call themselves the Society of the Sacred Heart of Jesus (when it became safe). Religious congregations were still outlawed in France.

When Mother Barat first came to visit Philippine at Ste. Marie, Philippine knelt and kissed the feet of the young superior. She was so happy and honored to have Mother Barat come to her humble monastery. The snow drifted in freely where doors and windows were still lacking. The cold was intense, and there were no means of heating many parts of the building. In the community room, an open fireplace gave a cheery glow as the nuns sat together for spiritual reading or at recreation, and small charcoal braziers were sometimes lit in their sleeping quarters, or hot bricks were placed in the beds to ensure warmth enough for sleep.

To Philippine, this was not a sacrifice. She was accustomed to the situation, but the other sisters didn't feel the same way, especially the ones who had known the old monastery before the war. Mother Barat and the other sisters accepted the conditions as a source of suffering with joy and generous love. Soon Mother Barat would begin her training of the sisters under the rule of the Society of the Sacred Heart of Jesus. The monastery would prove to be very difficult to continue. Philippine felt she was a failure

because she loved the old monastery. She now would leave it and join Mother Barat with her work.

Mother Barat had Philippine come to Paris to help her with the administration of all the convents, because the Society of the Sacred Heart was opening convents all over France. Philippine, now secretary general and treasurer, was entrusted with purchasing the property for a convent and school in Paris and with preparing and organizing the new convent at 40 Rue des Postes.

At the new convent, Philippine was seen directing the workmen, scrubbing and polishing the floors, occasionally inserting missing glass windowpanes, and even picking up a paint brush to whitewash walls. Once she was observed picking up a trowel to speed the mason's job. She was a tireless worker. This trait would be evident throughout her life.

Eleven sisters pronounced their vows before Communion at Mass in the chapel of the Franciscans in Rue de Grenville at the Convent of St. Thomas while they were waiting for their new convent to be completed.

The new schools run by the Society of the Sacred Heart of Jesus would be called academies. Their purpose was religious instruction and character formation. The elementary students studied religion, reading, spelling, writing, and courtesy. The next four years stressed grammar, geography, history, arithmetic, rhetoric, and literature. They also learned domestic economy, needlework, drawing, painting, singing, and instrumental music.

While in Paris, Philippine met many Jesuit missionary priests. Her heart yearned to go to the missions and teach the savages about Jesus. She asked Mother Barat's consent. She was told that she was needed in France to help the Society of the Sacred Heart of Jesus but not to give up hope.

Mother Barat told Philippine to wait. "Your time has not yet come."

Finally after twelve years of praying and hoping to go to the New World, in 1817, Bishop William Valentine DuBourg, bishop of Louisiana, came to visit the convent to ask for help for his American missions. Philippine threw herself at his feet and begged to be invited to the missions.

"God's hour has come. Do not let slip this chance. You have but to say the word. Say it. I beg you."

The bishop and Mother Barat told her they would consider her request. Philippine spent the night before the Blessed Sacrament, praying that God would want her to serve Him in the missions. Philippine was finally given permission to go to the missions in the Illinois Territory of America. She and her companions were to aid in the establishment of Catholic life in the Mississippi Valley.

Mother Barat commissioned Philippine. "If you only go to America to open one tabernacle to the Sacred Heart, will it not be enough for your happiness?"

Mother Philippine Duchesne, along with four others—Mother Octavie Berthold, Mother Eugenie Audé, Sister Catherine Lamarre, and Sister Marguerite Manteau—left for America from Bordeaux, France. Reverend Martial and Everemond Harissart, a seminarian, accompanied them. The four-mast clipper ship, *Rebecca*, spent seventy days at sea, fifty-two of those days out of sight of land.

Pirates from Buenos Aires approached their ship but left them alone after discovering it to be an American clipper. Nearly everyone on board the ship got very sick. There were terrific storms, torrential rains, violent headwinds, and excessive heat and then long periods of calm, which meant that they just drifted instead of sailed. At one point, the sailors said they should throw the sisters overboard because they were having such bad luck on the ship.

On May 25, 1818, they finally arrived near New Orleans, Louisiana. They were lifted off the ship in armchairs and into pirogues to go the rest of the way to New Orleans. There, on American soil for the first time, Philippine knelt and kissed the ground.

Everyone was sick with scurvy, especially Mother Duchesne. The good Ursuline Sisters on Chartres Street had the new arrivals stay with them to regain their health and strength. The Ursulines were so happy to have the five new sisters from France that they asked them to stay and open a school in New Orleans, where there were many Catholics.

Mother Gerard OSU was the infirmarian who nursed Mother Duchesne back to health. Sick as she was, Mother Duchesne used much of her time to write to her friends and family, whom she already missed, to tell them all about their trip so far. Father Louis Sibourd was the chaplain at the Ursuline Convent. He told her about the new country and what it would be like going up the Mississippi River.

Mother St. Michael OSU, the superior of the convent, was so helpful and generous to Philippine and her companions. She paid the $500 for the steamboat tickets for the sisters to go to St. Louis and gave them an extra $300 for anything they might need on their trip and upon their arrival in St. Louis. Their luggage and packages contained a picture of the Sacred Heart; one of St. Francis Regis, her patron; and a statue of Our Lady.

The trip on the paddle steamer, *The Franklin*, took forty days because it had to stop often for firewood and they had to chop down the trees. Philippine saw Native Americans for the first time. They were riding horseback. She was excited to see them because she thought she had come to teach the Native Americans about the God who loved them. But when she arrived in St.

Louis, she would find the only Native Americans adults who were traders. There were no children until later at Florissant.

Upon her arrival, Philippine was told that the bishop did not have any place for them to stay or start a school but that they might room for a while with General Pratte and his family. There was not an empty shelter or house in the city. Nor was there a hotel. The crowding came from many new settlers and fur traders in the city. St. Louis had three banks by then: the Bank of Missouri, Bank of St. Louis, and St. Louis Exchange Bank. Also the American Fur Company had its Western headquarters there. The Missouri River flowed into the Mississippi River not far from the city. It was a crossroads of the country.

The bishop rented a house in St. Charles, across the Missouri River, made of upright white oak logs. It had a slanted shingled roof, which extended five feet over a gallery that ran the length of the house, front and back. He was renting from Widow Duquette, who stayed in the house, along with the sisters and their students. The house had six small rooms that opened onto a large central living room. The Duquette Mansion on Second Street at Decatur provided a temporary but very unsatisfactory location in which to begin their first school.

This school would be the first free school just west of where the Missouri meets the Mississippi River. More importantly, it would be the first tabernacle in the first Convent of the Sacred Heart in the New World. The first Mass would be said on September 8, 1818, at the Duquette Mansion. Before long, they had twenty pupils in the free school.

In October, Emelie and Celeste Pratte and Pelagie Chouteau came from St. Louis to become the first boarders. Later, six day scholars would join in their studies at the new academy. The students learned to read, do arithmetic, and sew. More importantly, they learned to love the Sacred Heart. Mother Audé

was especially popular with the children. She taught astronomy, geography, songs, and traditions of the Sacré Coeur in France. Prizes were distributed at the closing of the year. Ribbons were given for academic merit and for conduct. That school year ended on August 31, 1819.

The parents from St. Louis and many other parents felt St. Charles was too far away, especially in the winter when it was difficult to cross the Missouri River. St. Charles was very cold that winter of 1818. Even the milk froze in the kitchen and had to be chipped and thawed before drinking. Mother Audé had a very cold job milking the cow. There was a bread shortage. Not even cornmeal was for sale in the village. The Duquette well went dry, and the streams nearby were muddied by animals or frozen over. With very little money to buy food, the sisters went hungry often. Mother Duchesne wrote that she sometimes became light-headed with hunger.

As they had arrived in September, the sisters did not have many vegetables but ate apples, plums, and pears from their garden that first winter. Some people paid the dollar-a-month tuition in currency, and some parents bartered instead with a load of wood, a bucket of water, a sack of corn, six pounds of butter, three dinner plates, measures of sugar, two turkeys, a day's work in the garden, or help with the washing. Cabbage and potatoes were a common lunch.

At times, they had to pay twelve cents a bucket for water when everything was frozen. Once spring came, the sisters and pupils put in a garden. Once the vegetables were ready to pick, Mother Duchesne had the girls help her again in the garden. Mother Duchesne would dig up the potatoes, and the girls would follow behind her and collect them.

The boarders from St. Louis had many pretty dresses when they came to school. Mother Duchesne was busy many nights

mending the girls' and the sisters' clothing and making vestments for the priests who worked in the missions. Part of the training and education of the girls was sewing. The girls shared the rare needles and scissors and soon ran out of thread and material. Much of the sewing material was sent by relatives and friends from France at Philippine's request. She was always asking for needles and cloth for the girls and herself to make the priests' clothing.

After much difficulty, in 1819 Mother Duchesne moved her five sisters and five boarders to the bishop's farm in Florissant, Missouri. They loaded all their belonging, including the animals and the three paintings, onto carts and then unloaded them onto a flat-bottomed boat called a *groupato* to cross the Missouri River. Then they put them back onto carts again for the walk to Florissant.

What a sight: cows, calves, and chickens! They made seventeen trips back and forth to St. Charles before they were settled into the Florissant farmhouse. Mother Duchesne's cows refused to cooperate, so she put cabbages on the top and sides of the three carts to entice the cows to follow her. She let them eat the cabbages once they crossed the river at Florissant.

Reverend Marie-Joseph Dunand, a Trappist priest who had been in Florissant for many years, was happy to have the sisters. He raised the money to build a new church, and the pious Irish men of the area built it in time to celebrate Christmas Eve Mass. How proud these Irish men were to have built a beautiful house of God in the wilderness. The new church was dedicated to the Sacred Heart. Philippine was always very indebted to Father Dunand.

Their one-room log cabin or farmhouse with its two windows and fireplace served as a dormitory, refectory (dining room), parlor, and classroom. At night, the students and sisters rolled out buffalo

robes and blankets to make their beds. The first new novices of the society in America—Mathilde Hamilton, Virginia Labadie, Emilie Rolette, Betsie Rolette, and Mary Layton—had to sleep upstairs in the loft. This cabin was two miles from the church, a long walk on cold days. They frequently had to gather wood in the forest, as they did not have servants or helpers. Sometimes, if guests were at the convent, they had to burn their entire supply of firewood in one day because the Americans expected a roaring fire.

Father Charles DeLa Croix, who had been living in the cabin before the sisters arrived, moved out and slept in a corncrib. This proved to be very unhealthy, as he developed a fever and became very ill from the cold, for "the crib was as open as a birdcage." The bishop ordered a new cabin to be built for Father DeLa Croix when he heard how sick the priest was.

In Florissant, Mother Berthold was put in charge of the day students. Mother Audé was entrusted with the boarders, and Mother Duchesne taught religion and trained the new novices for the Society of the Sacred Heart. Mother Duchesne never learned English well enough to teach in the language but was able to work with the many French students and teach mathematics and Latin. Letters tell us that the girls wore uniforms in Florissant that were pink magenta trimmed in black velvet.

The goodness of the Ursuline Sisters continued over the next few years. They sent Mother Philippine barrels of rice, sugar, codfish, raisins, and preserves from New Orleans by way of steamboat. Philippine and the sisters were ever so grateful.

In 1820, twenty-six men built a real schoolhouse for the sisters. They did it all in one day. It was called a house raising. Mother Duchesne had borrowed 10,000 francs, about $2,000 from Mr. John Mullanphy at 10 percent interest. The bishop advised her to do it. The new convent and school were ready within a very

short time. They had discussed it in November and finished it on December 23. Philippine had begged St. Thomas the Apostle, St. Regis, and St. Francis Xavier to obtain for her and the sisters the grace that all their labor might be for the glory of the Sacred Hearts of Jesus and Mary.

The sisters and the older girls trudged the two miles in the snow to their new convent. After hauling all the furnishings and the little children with their bundles, Mothers Duchesne and Eugenie set out to get the last cow to join the rest. This cow had never let them lead her with a rope, so Philippine filled her apron with corn in order to coax her to follow. The cow preferred her liberty and ran headlong into the bushes and trees along the path. They tried to keep up with her, but the two sisters floundered several times in the snow, tearing their habits on the brambles. By now, the sisters had six cows, and Mother Eugenie Audé was still in charge of milking. Florissant had rich soil, and the sisters made a good garden for themselves.

In these early years at Florissant, when Mother Duchesne was teaching the French girls, one of the young women wrote about Mother Duchesne, the teacher. She looked at Mother Duchesne as the perfect model of all virtues. In more than two years as class mistress, never once did Mother Duchesne lack poise or self-control. Nor did she act with the least air of impatience in dealing with the group of children who were so difficult to handle. She showed the same gentle kindliness toward all.

Bishop DuBourg proposed another convent in Louisiana. A very rich widow, Mrs. Charles Smith, in Opelousas, Louisiana, would pay for the transportation and support of sisters from France and would donate the land, house, and furniture, plus the servants.

The new convent, sixty leagues from New Orleans, was called Grand Coteau (Big Hill). Mother Duchesne was delighted to

spread devotion to the Sacred Heart of Jesus and set up a new altar in His honor. Bishop DuBourg insisted that Mother Eugenie Audé and Sr. Mary Layton be the sisters sent to Grand Coteau. They boarded the steamboat *Rapide* for their journey.

The new school in the South prospered while times were very hard for the people in Florissant because the Bank of Missouri failed and many parents could not even pay tuition. Mother Duchesne didn't want the children to leave school, for she feared they would lose their faith. Therefore, they sacrificed and shared what little they had. Grand Coteau and Philippine's family sent them some money.

Eighteen twenty-one was a busy year. Father Henri Pratte brought a new postulant, Judith Labruyere, to Florissant from Ste. Genevieve. Mother Lucille Mathevon went to Florissant, and Mother Xavier Murphy went to the newly opened Grand Coteau. This was the second Convent of the Sacred Heart in America.

Also that year, Father John Acquaroni, a missionary at Portage des Sioux, visited Florissant. Imagine how excited Philippine was, for she thought a missionary to the Native Americans was very special. The father told Philippine about his work. She sat down and wrote to Mother Barat about how she had enough new novices and could afford to send a couple of sisters to work with the Native Americans at Portage des Sioux. There was no reply. Many times letters were not received because they were lost in transit. There was no way to know unless someone found the letter.

In 1823, Philippine took a trip to visit her new convents, Grand Coteau and St. Michaels, also on the Mississippi. The trip began on the *Heckla* and took sixty-three days, although she was only at Grand Coteau for fourteen days. On the return trip up the Mississippi River, many people caught yellow fever on the riverboat, and thirteen people died. Mother Duchesne got

sick, and they told her to get off the boat at Natchez, Tennessee. There, her companion, Therese Pratte, found a room for her in a widower's home. His wife had just died three weeks earlier, and he had not even changed her bed linens.

June 1823 was a happier time. The Jesuits arrived. Father Charles Felix Van Quickenborne, SJ, came with Brothers Henry Reiselman and Peter de Meyer and three African American couples, Tom and Molly, Moses and Nancy, and Issas and Succy. Philippine made cassocks for Jesuit missionaries from the sisters' choir cloaks. She also sewed together liturgical robes for them to take to their missions.

By this time, the sisters in Florissant had a hundred chickens, seven cows, nine hogs, and one horse. Philippine cared for the swine. She didn't think that was very pleasant, but someone had to do it.

Unfortunately the pleasant picture changed. Florissant was again flooded, and many farms were ruined, along with all the vegetables. Water surrounded the convent as the house stood between two creeks that rose over their banks. Water washed away the gardens and yards several times. When this happened, the Jesuit priests had to swim across with their horses in order to offer Mass. Once, the father's horse arrived without the rider, and the sisters worried that he had drowned. Eventually he came, soaked from head to foot. His horse had thrown him.

With the gardens gone, the main support of the entire community was gone. Mother Barat proposed to close Florissant, but Philippine fought to keep it open. Philippine would not get discouraged even if they had only seven boarders and three orphans. Once the water went down, they still had their cows, and they reasoned that with winter coming on, firewood was still cheaper in Florissant than St. Louis.

In 1825, Father Van Quickenborne arrived with two little Native American girls. This would be the birth of the Female Indian Seminary. Mother O'Connor was put in charge of the girls. By 1826, Philippine had ten Native American boys and six Native American girls at Florissant.

On April 17, Mother Mathilde Hamilton was professed as the first American Religious of the Sacred Heart. She received her gold ring of perpetual espousal and the silver cross of full membership in the Society of the Sacred Heart.

More Jesuits arrived from Europe. Father John Théodore de Théaux, SJ, and Brother John O'Connor, SJ, visited St. Ferdinand in Florissant upon their arrival.

After the Academy of the Sacred Heart, St. Michael's was opened, and soon another academy was opened at Bayou la Fourche in the lower Mississippi Valley. Mother Emilie Audé was put in charge of the convent. Mother Mathilde Hamilton; Sisters Mullanphy, Labruyere, and Timon; and three more novices from Grand Coteau joined the community that taught at St. Michaels. Mother Xavier Murphy, assisted by Mother Carmelite Landry, was named the superior of Grand Coteau, Louisiana. Back in Florissant, Anna Shannon and Suzanne McKay entered the novitiate and later became known as Sisters Stanislaus and Aloysia.

In 1827, Mr. John Mullanphy, a successful immigrant from Ireland, agreed to lease twenty-four acres and a large house to Philippine rent-free, with the costly stipulation that they always care for fifteen to twenty orphans. He and his heirs would contribute five dollars a year for each of the students. These were the first students of City House.

A month later, six boarders came. City House was the first free school for girls in St. Louis. By the end of the year, they had thirty students in their free school and ten paying students in the

day school, only twelve boarders and eight mulatto children in Sunday school.

The essential things taught at the academy were devotion to the Sacred Heart and spiritual, intellectual, and moral training. Mother Duchesne was the superior and treasurer. She wrote about how some parents could not pay the tuition when times were hard. Father Saulnier, pastor of the Cathedral of St. Louis, donated desks and benches from the closed St. Louis College. He also gave her a cow. This was much needed and appreciated.

Mother Duchesne also held the office of mistress general and surveillante and taught five religion classes. By May 18, 1829, Philippine had one hundred students and four postulants in her newest convent, the Academy of the Sacred Heart, City House, in St. Louis.

In 1828, the convent, Academy of the Sacred Heart in St. Charles, Missouri, had reopened with the promise of the Jesuits to build a school building. Mothers Mary O'Connor and Lucille Mathevon were chosen to direct the convent and school. When Philippine first returned with the sisters to Duquette House, the living room floor had rotted and fallen in to the lower level, where hogs and sheep had found shelter for the past few years. The atmosphere was foul with musty dampness and decay. Window frames and glass and doors had to be replaced. Village carpenters closed the gaping holes in the roof and the floor and replaced the stones in the foundation that the animal intruders had pushed away.

With the aid of a Native American woman, who had come with the nuns from Florisssant, they soon had the place presentable. Mass was celebrated the second day in the central room, and Bishop Rosati, along with twelve Jesuits, chanted the "Office of the Dedication of a Church." A new church was built later. The

Jesuits funded the building of a new two-story schoolhouse. They soon added a third story to the building.

By 1830, there were six institutions run by the Society in America, with more than 350 children being taught by some 64 nuns. Fourteen had come from France, and 50 were Americans. Three sisters had died in the twelve years Philippine had been in America.

The winter of 1830/31 brought much physical suffering to Florissant. The snow was so deep that the cattle died from exposure and starvation. There was a shortage of fuel, and many people got very sick from the cold. Philippine nursed her sick sisters and students. The good news that season came from France, where her cousin Casmir Périer was elected prime minister of France.

That summer was terribly hot in Florissant, and many got ill. Philippine again was very busy nursing the sick. She spent eleven nights in a row staying up with one of her very sick religious sisters.

Cholera struck again in October 1832, and hundreds died in St. Louis alone. Parents and Philippine were very happy that none of the students had gotten sick or died. This epidemic was spreading in Europe and in the United States.

Even Bishop Rosati became very ill, but he did not die. He did, however, come to visit less often because he was so busy with the responsibilities of his large diocese. Mother Philippine missed his guidance. Once, Bishop Rosati brought the bishop of Bardstown, Kentucky, Bishop Benedict Joseph Flaget, to visit the convent, and Bishop Rosati asked Mother Philippine to make the visitor a cassock from the purple silk cloth that she had on hand. She did of course.

In 1834, Mother Philippine left City House and returned to the Academy of the Sacred Heart in Florissant. She felt so useless because she thought she was too old to help anyone. Now

she prayed all the time and did every thankless job. She woke the religious in the morning, cleaned out the outhouses, did the scrubbing and sweeping, and of course nursed the sick and suffering sisters. She denied herself any comfort and slept in a little room under the staircase that was across from the chapel. She loved being so near the chapel. She attended all the masses and loved giving the responses to the priests. She was known to carry her mattress around to the different rooms of the sick and sleep with them so they wouldn't be alone.

In 1834, a terrible fire on the riverfront in St. Louis did some damage to the St. Louis Cathedral. Bishop Rosati was desperate. Philippine gave him some money to repair some of the damages. What little she had, she shared, and if it were money or herself, she was always happy to do things to help others.

Mother Philippine missed her friends in France, especially her family. She prayed for all of them in France and America. Mother Stanislaus Shannon wrote about the day that while walking in the convent's garden and looking at the onions, potatoes, and other common vegetables, she saw Mother Duchesne trimming off the edges of the cabbages with one hand and holding a rosary in the other, trying to brush away the tears that were running down her cheeks. She sat there on a boulder by the path, overcome by deep sorrow. Mother Duchesne often thought she was a failure and useless to her community because she didn't speak English well.

Philippine would wear worn-out clothing and was said to be a sight to behold. Her patched habit and veil were her joy. She loved poverty, claiming it was a matter of personal taste as well as a means of imitating the Poor Man of Nazareth. Some referred to her as the Francis of Assisi of the Society. She was sensitive to the cold but refused the luxury of a fire in her room except when ill.

She ate stale bread and drank weak coffee for breakfast at seventy years of age. She was always at work mending, if time

allowed. She would slip around at night and check the religious and the children's clothing, and she'd carry off the mending and repair it or replace it with fresh clothes. The children never seemed to figure out how this happened. She often brought her sewing with her as she sat with the sick.

Her favorite pastime was reading mail from France, especially from her dear Superior Mother Madeline Sophie Barat, her sister Euphrosine, and her cousin Josephine.

Finally in 1840, at the age of seventy-two, Mother Duchesne survived another almost fatal illness, thanks to the loving care of Mothers Stanislaus and Judith and Regis Hamilton. The Holy Father, Pope Gregory VII, said he would like to see the Religious of the Sacred Heart work among the Native Americans. Father Peter DeSmet, SJ, also pleaded with Mother Barat to send some sisters among the Native Americans.

Bishop Rosati, in France on business, asked Mother Barat to send Philippine to the Potowatomi Mission in Sugar Creek, Kansas. Many of the Native Americans were Christian and wished to learn more about God. Philippine would be very welcome and safe there. Philippine's dream was finally to come true.

Philippine repeated her favorite prayer upon hearing of her mission. "Lord, I lean on you alone for strength. Give me your arm to support me, your shoulders to carry me, your breast on which to lay my head, your cross to uphold me, and your Eucharist to nourish me. In you, Lord, I shall sleep and rest in peace."

Mother Duchesne was apparently too weak to make the journey to Kansas, but Father Verhaegen, SJ, insisted that she be taken along, even though he knew how much she was suffering. He said, "Even if she can use only one leg, she will come. Why, if we have to carry her all the way on our shoulders, she is coming with us. She may not be able to do much work, but she will draw down all manner of heavenly favors on the work."

On June 29, 1841, Mothers Philippine Duchesne, Lucille Mathevon, and Mary Ann O'Connor and Sister Louise Amyote started on their trip. The trip was very smooth. They traveled up the Missouri River on the steamboat *Emilie* for four days until they arrived at Westport. They passed fifteen towns on their way and were surprised to see thousands of inhabitants in each. The other travelers in the party were Fathers Verhaegen, Jean Baptiste Smedt, and Francis J. Renaud, and an African American named Edmund.

About a mile from the mission house, a band of five hundred Native American braves appeared in gala dress: bright blankets, plumes and feathers, and moccasins embroidered with porcupine quills. Their faces were painted black with red circles around the eyes that gave them a frighteningly grotesque appearance. As the mission wagon advanced, the Native Americans performed a series of equestrian drills, now in semicircles, then in circles, and always with such precision that never was a horse out of position.

The Native Americans, impatient for the sisters' arrival, sent two members ahead who knelt and asked for Father Superior's blessing. Philippine wrote to Mother Barat,

> These Indians had been driven out of Michigan by the Americans. Half of their number were baptized Catholics. They built their village away from the other Indians who were pagan. Once baptized, they never reverted to drunkness or stealing. Whatever is found is placed at the door of the church to be claimed by its owner. Not a single house has locks on the doors, yet nothing is ever missing. The Indians gathered in groups (men and women separate) and say morning

prayers, attend Mass, and learn more catechism. In the evening they assemble again for prayers.

Even though Philippine couldn't teach the Native American children as Mother O'Connor did, cook as Mother Louise did, or read the language as Mother Mathevon did, they loved her and respected "the good old lady," as they referred to her. They brought her all manner of things: fresh corn, newly laid eggs, chickens, wild plums, and sweet, clean straw for her pallet.

Often Philippine stayed all morning in the church, so Sister Louise would take her a cup of coffee each day, and she would drink it at the door of the church. After dinner, she went again for three or four hours of prayer. The Native Americans had the greatest admiration for her, recommended themselves to her prayers, and called her "woman who prays always."

Mother Duchesne was so happy on Sundays to inscribe in the register the names of the men and women baptized that day. Yet she felt she had not achieved anything herself. She still felt she had failed. She didn't realize that her example was so very important. Her inability to do active work brought her loneliness of heart, which she admitted and accepted with love but not without pain. The solitude at Sugar Creek was not merely a physical remoteness, but also a spiritual aloneness that grew out of the sensed fact that she was a burden on those who cared for her and an anxiety for them. Borne in close union with the mystery of Christ's loneliness, this suffering only drew her closer to His sacred heart, where she buried the pain by renewed and more loving surrender.

The Potawatomi language was extremely difficult for Philippine. Their alphabet had four letters less than the French did. Many of the words had eight and ten syllables, and there was no published dictionary to help Philippine pronounce the words.

The only words that she mastered were *God, man, woman, sun, moon, salt, fire,* and *finger.*

Much of the time, Philippine lay on her bed, praying or knitting stockings. Her companions were very concerned for her. But she was content just to die among the Native Americans. Mother Barat would not accept this, and after only a year, Mother Duchesne was ordered to return to Missouri, to whichever convent she chose to live. The sisters had some twenty Native American girls in their school and felt they were being successful. There were at least a hundred Native Americans at Mass and Holy Communion on Sunday, and they didn't drink or gamble. At least four hundred Catholic Native Americans attended Mass on Christmas. The charity among the Native Americans was very noticeable, and many families said the rosary with each member having his or her own rosary beads.

The log chapel was completed at Sugar Creek, Kansas, and dedicated to the Blessed Mother. It was blessed under the title of Immaculate Conception of the Blessed Virgin. When Philippine was stronger, she would kneel in the new chapel and not move for hours at a time. The Native American children wondered if she ever moved while at prayer. The children put petals on her habit one evening while she was at silent prayer and returned in the morning to see that she had not moved. The children would noiselessly approach her, kneel, and kiss the hem of her worn habit or the fringe of her shawl or skirt. To them, she was *Quah-Kah-Ka-Num-ad* (woman who prays always).

Father Verhaegen accompanied Mother Philippine back to St. Louis, where she rested before Mother Gray escorted her to St. Charles. There again through a lifetime habit, she accepted God's will through love. The loving kindness helped to lessen the sorrow that weighed heavily upon her. In the quiet routine of St. Charles, the realization of failure crept over her once more,

bringing with it an agony of disappointment that summed itself up in the haunting thought.

"All that effort of love in vain," she wrote to her cousin Josephine.

But she knew in her heart that it had not been in vain, and peace came flooding into her soul as she knelt in the cloister chapel and renewed her complete surrender to God's will. She would never teach the Native American children as she had dreamed. Instead she would take her place in her community and see to the welfare of the others around her there in St. Charles and at the other American convents. One of the first things she did was to write to others, asking them to please send money to the Propagation of Faith in care of the Provincial of the Jesuits to help the Native American missions.

Mother Duchesne's room was a small room toward the end of the chapel, about eight feet wide and fifteen feet long. It was furnished with a cot, a chair, a wooden box in which she kept her treasures, a prie-dieu (a piece of furniture for use during prayer, consisting of a kneeling surface and a narrow upright front with a rest for the elbows or books), some letters of Mother General Barat, and a few spiritual notebooks. There were also two or three old pictures of pious subjects on the walls and some well-worn prayer books on the little table.

In St. Charles, Philippine could sit at the window sewing when she wasn't supervising the parish school and look out to see the turbulent Missouri River and the rolling country beyond. From the back porch of the convent, she could look up the hillside and see the dilapidated, old Duquette Mansion, now a washhouse. Often she could see the children in their pink gingham uniforms and green sunbonnets playing on the gallery of the house or under the big trees on the playground. At a short distance from

the church, she could see the little cemetery where Mother Eulalie Guillot was buried.

The work of the Society was continuing, and Mother Duchesne took particular interest in the convents in New York and Pennsylvania because she knew the religious personally. They were her former students or novices from Florissant and Grand Coteau.

In 1843, many were taken ill with yellow fever, and the children at St. Charles were transferred to St. Ferdinand in Florissant, leaving just eight religious at St. Charles. They offered their convent to the Visitandine religious at Kaskaskia who needed to leave the island because of the terrible flooding. They didn't accept the offer because they wanted to establish a monastery nearer St. Louis. This would be the Visitation Academy, now moved to Ballas Rd. in West County of St. Louis, MO. This one block from academy of the Sacred Heart villa duchesne-Oak Hill School this is a Pre-K through sixth grade for boys and girls. Today Academy of the Sacred Heart in St. Charles is also co-ed Pre-K for sixth grade.

The Academy of the Sacred Heart in St. Charles reopened the following year with Mother Hamilton as the superior in 1844. Mother Galitzin, Mother Barat's secretary in Paris, informed the American religious that Mother Barat, their superior general, was a very busy woman and that everyone should refrain from writing her letters unless it concerned important business. This was a terrible burden for Philippine, for she loved to write to her friend and spiritual mother and was accustomed to receiving warm, charming, and deeply spiritual letters from her in return. But the knowledge that St. Charles was to continue its apostolate brightened her outlook, and her pen was often busy with letters to her family and to other religious and priests.

In the spring of 1845, the worst flood on the Missouri River ever known caused tremendous destruction, and many families lost everything—homes, furniture, cattle, crops, and harvest. The people in St. Louis were very generous and took families into their homes. Some individuals, not particularly rich people, took in as many as seven sick families that came from the flooded districts of Illinois and provided for all their needs for over six months.

Mother Duchesne had regained her strength. She was feeling better physically, and her mind was much clearer. She was the principal of the parish school in St. Charles for there were still French-speaking children at St. Charles. Her solitude was brightened—"sweetened" wrote a member of the community— by the fact that she could always be close to Jesus in the Blessed Sacrament. He had not forsaken "His poor servant," as she called herself. More than ever, she experienced the sweetness and joy of His presence.

Besides the long hours she spent in adoration, she had the privilege of giving the Latin responses at all the masses offered in the church or the cloister chapel, for acolytes (altar boys/girls today) were few and unreliable. Even at the age of eighty years, she continued to do this, kneeling upright without support, not only during one Mass but during several offered in succession. She was also very punctual about the private recitation of office to the very last days of her life.

She heard from Josephine de Savoye-Rollin on her seventy-sixth birthday and received a gift of money and a package. But the most welcome gift was the news of her family. Philippine was sad that she had not heard from Mother Barat, and she asked if any letters had been lost. Philippine was desolate now in 1846, for she feared that the friend whom she loved more than anyone else on earth was displeased with her.

In her humility, she attributed this silence to some serious fault on her part, yet the most searching self-examination failed to reveal any action that could have merited such punishment. She remained hopeful that she would hear from her Mother General Madeline Sophie Barat.

For several months, Mother Barat was wondering why she hadn't heard from Philippine. Puzzled by this silence and the reports from others, Mother Barat determined to set this matter right by the most acceptable means in her power. She sent Mother Amelie Jouve, Mother Philippine's niece, personally to give her love and explain the terrible mistake. Mother Jouve gave an account of her visit with her Tante Philippine. Mother Duchesne received the fortunate niece as an angel from heaven.

After reading the letter sent to her by our Reverend Mother General, her dearest friend, she seemed transported with joy. Tears flowed down her cheeks, and she was speechless with emotion. After a little while, she exclaimed, "So our Mother General still thinks of me, still loves me? She has been so good as to show me that love by sending you to visit me." She was radiant with joy.

During her visit, Mother Jouve did her best to discover what would give pleasure to her dear old aunt or what had caused her pain. Neither pleasure nor pain seemed of interest to her then. She had the assurance of the unaltered love of her dearest friend, and that was enough. Mother Jouve assured Philippine that letters from Mother Madeline Sophie had certainly gone astray. Philippine knew this could certainly be true.

Mother Amelie Jouve's visit to St. Charles lasted but two weeks. During this time, she was able to persuade her Tante Philippine to wear a warm shawl by day and a woolen camisole by night and to take a bit of meat more often. They had a wonderful time talking about family and friends.

In 1850, Mother Philippine wrote to Father De La Croix about the twelve convents of the Sacred Heart, the fire in St. Louis's riverfront, and the cholera epidemic that followed. She told him that she was eighty-one and had been in America for thirty-one years and had accomplished little for the Good Master. She asked Father to pray for her and to please offer a Mass for her happy death. She told him she had a new superior and asked for his blessing on both of them for the love of the heart of Jesus.

Philippine was able to be very busy that winter and spring, preparing useful articles of clothing and sacristy supplies for missionaries, and offered them to Father Peter De Smet, SJ, when he visited that year.

The notice of the death of Father Joseph Varin, SJ, in France saddened Mother Duchesne and all the religious. He had introduced Mother Madeline Sophie Barat to Mother Philippine Duchesne fifty years before. Mother Duchesne found out about his illness from a Kentucky newspaper. The paper noted that Father Joseph Desire Varin had been the author of the "Constitutions for the Religious of the Sacred Heart." Mother Duchesne wrote to Mother Barat to share her sorrow and loss.

When the Society of the Sacred Heart celebrated its golden jubilee on November 21, 1850, it counted 2,055 religious, living in 65 convents scattered through France, Italy, Belgium, Austria, England, Ireland, Canada, and the United States.

Early in 1851, Philippine began to experience sudden attacks of weakness. In August, she gave no evidence of mental confusion in the letter, which she addressed to Mother Barat. It ended with,

> After telling you our problems, I beg you to sustain this house. Do not treat it as Florissant was treated. In spite of all the difficulties, we shall

always have day pupils who pay a little, the poor
children who have no other chance for education,
and some boarding pupils from the vicinity and
even from St. Louis, as we have at present, and
they pay very well.

Philippine had pleaded for the return of Mother Hamilton
to St. Charles from Canada. She had been there for almost four
years, and Philippine missed her. In November 1851, Mother
Hamilton returned and was saddened to see how Philippine could
scarcely walk or make herself be heard. Philippine asked Mother
Hamilton if she wanted to sleep in her room with her. Mother
Hamilton was overjoyed to be able to dress and care for Mother
Philippine Duchesne.

Throughout the winter and spring of 1852, Philippine seemed
to gain strength and resumed writing letters to friends and family.
She was alert to all that concerned her in the community and
school, the Native American missions, and the Society. She wrote
in a letter to her sister in June that she found herself stronger now
and had stopped calculating when she would meet death.

"It will be God's will. Old age has many sacrifices to make,
and it can be a period of great value as one's purgatory. It will
certainly be a less rigorous one than that of the next life."

With characteristic determination, Philippine resolved to
make the community retreat but developed a high fever. On
August 16, 1852, she asked for the last sacraments. Father
Verhaegen, SJ, came and anointed her. She thanked him with
a radiant smile. Next day she was better and wrote three little
notes to bid adieu to all she loved best in this world: the Society
and its foundress, Madeline Sophie Barat; her family; the Native
American missions; and Father De Smet, SJ.

Mother Duchesne grew weaker every day. Each morning she went to chapel carried by the religious. She would sit close to the sanctuary railing. It was the Mass that mattered, and Holy Communion was her daily bread. Now feeble and tottering, she was bent, showing her gaunt frame clothed in patched garments. Her once-luminous eyes now dimmed. She might have evoked pity from a stranger who saw her seated there. But her sisters in religion looked on her with awed love and veneration, knowing the truth of which she was unconscious, reverencing the sanctity of which she was unaware. Her message to them, though unspoken, was a message of lively faith. She had put God first in her life because she had realized with astounding clarity that He is first and also last, Alpha and Omega, and that between Him and all else in the universe there is, there can be no comparison.

After the Holy Sacrifice, she was taken back to her little room to spend the rest of the morning in quiet prayer before returning to the chapel for adoration in the afternoon. She had written a prayer in a spiritual notebook years before and had kept it for nearly thirty-five years.

> O my God, I desire to live as a victim offered in a spirit of penance and love. Then let me prepare all that is needed for a sacrifice of love whose perfume will rise even to the Heart of Jesus. May my whole being be the victim, all that I am and all that I have. May my own heart be the altar, my separation from the world and all earthly pleasures the sacrificial knife. May my love be the consuming fire, and my yearning desires the breeze that fans it. Let me pour on it the incense and perfume of all virtues, and to this mystical sacrifice let me bring all that I cling to, that I

may offer all, burn all, consume all, keeping back nothing for self. O Divine Love, my very God, accept this sacrifice which I desire to offer You at every instant of my life.

On Tuesday, November 16, a knock on the convent door brought a welcomed personal messenger to Philippine once again from Mother Madeline Sophie Barat. Mother DuRousier came from France to bring Mother Barat's blessing and love to her beloved daughter in Christ. Mother DuRousier asked for a blessing from Mother Duchesne, and the dying saint raised her thin hand and traced a cross on Mother DuRousier's forehead.

"I still seem to feel the cross," Mother DuRousier said often afterward, "and I trust it will bring me happiness."

On the following day, Philippine was decidedly weaker and suffered from a cough that gave her no rest. Toward midnight, Mother Hamilton offered her a drink. Philippine refused, fearing to break her Eucharistic fast.

"Take it," urged Mother Hamilton. "It is not yet midnight."

"Are you sure?" replied Philippine.

In the hours before dawn, Father Verhaegen prepared to bring Holy Communion to Mother Philippine Duchesne.

When one of the sisters was preparing a fire in the room, Mother Duchesne reproached her and said, "You think only of material things. It would be better to say a Pater and Ave for the good of my soul."

Mother Hamilton then told her the religious were all praying in the adjoining room.

"Oh!" she exclaimed. "How fortunate I am to die in a house where such charity reigns!"

Mother Philippine Duchesne received the viaticum from Father Verhaegen, and after he had said Mass, he returned to anoint her again, for she was sinking rapidly.

She heard the invocation, "Jesus, Mary, Joseph." And she answered audibly, "I give you my heart, my soul, and my life. Oh yes, my life generously."

It was noon as the Angelus ceased ringing. The heroic life of Mere Duchesne came to an end.

P. J. Verhaegen, SJ, wrote, "Eminent in all virtues of religious life, but especially in humility, she sweetly and calmly departed this life in the odor of sanctity on the 18th day of November, 1852."

St. John Paul II canonized Rose Philippine Duchesne, RSCJ, on July 3, 1988, only after St. Madeline Sophie Barat, RSCJ, was canonized on May 24, 1925.

Printed and bound by PG in the USA